Intelligence Information

Thinking

About the Author

Edward de Bono has been called 'the father of thinking about thinking'. He is the originator of the concept – and formal tools – of Lateral Thinking. He is regarded by many as the leading authority in the field of creative thinking, innovation and the direct teaching of thinking as a skill.

His methods are taught in thousands of schools around the world and his instruction in thinking has been sought by many business organisations over the years, including IBM, Prudential, Shell, Nokia, Bank of America and GM. He is on the Accenture list of the fifty most influential business thinkers in the world.

Dr de Bono was born in Malta. He was a Rhodes Scholar at Oxford, holds an M.A. in psychology and physiology from Oxford, a D. Phil. in Medicine, a Ph.D. from Cambridge, a D. Des. (Doctor of Design) from the Royal Melbourne Institute of Technology and an LL.D. from Dundee. He holds professorships at the Universities of Malta and Pretoria, Dublin City University and the University of Central England.

Intelligence
Information
Thinking

Edward de Bono
(inventor of lateral thinking)

BLACKHALL
PUBLISHING

This book was typeset by Ark Imaging for

BLACKHALL PUBLISHING
33 Carysfort Avenue
Blackrock
Co. Dublin
Ireland
e-mail: info@blackhallpublishing.com
www.blackhallpublishing.com

© 2007 The McQuaig Group, Inc.
ISBN 978-1-84218-133-1

A catalogue record for this book is available from
the British Library.

Printed in the United Kingdom by Cromwell Press

INTELLIGENCE

Intelligence is like the horsepower of a car.

Thinking is like the skill with which the car is driven.

Information is like the road map available to the driver.

Recently a taxi driver told me that his brother was an excellent fighter pilot but a very bad car driver.

The fighter pilot was excellent in control of his plane in a clear sky. This was a matter of control.

With a car driver the control is only one aspect. The behaviour of other drivers on the road is very important. The nature of the road itself is very important.

It can be the same with intelligent people.

We could define 'intelligence' as 'the ability to do well at IQ tests'.

If the performance on IQ tests does actually correlate with performance as an accountant or scientist then the IQ tests are a valid predictor for those fields.

The difficulty arises when the 'intelligence' part of the 'Intelligence Quotient' (IQ test) is taken as meaning the general use of the word 'intelligent'.

The original use of the IQ tests was a very valid one. The intention was to see how an individual child compared to the average for that age and background. Those children who were obviously below the average needed special attention.

The children who were below average might have been so because of an impaired mental capacity or because of their social background and a lack of stimulation at home. 'Culture free' tests were designed to try to remove the social effects.

There can be no doubt that IQ tests do measure a type of intelligence but is this the same as the general-purpose intelligence used in daily life?

There is evidence that IQ tests correlate well with the speed of transmission along the neurons in the brain. This itself is determined by enzyme kinetics.

There is endless argument about the relative contributions of genes and nurture to traditional IQ results.

The Intelligence Trap

There are some aspects of a high intelligence that become a sort of trap.

A person with a high intelligence can take a position on a subject and then use their intelligence to defend that position very ably. The better the defence of that position the less does that person see any need to consider alternatives or listen to others. That is not good thinking.

Someone who has grown up with the realisation that he or she is more intelligent than most people around wants to get the best reward for being so intelligent. The quickest and best reward is to prove other people wrong. This is a risk-free demonstration of superiority. It is also relatively easy.

An intelligent person takes in information quickly and can reach a conclusion in a short time. A less intelligent person has to wait to take in more information and may, occasionally, reach a better conclusion.

This is all like the driver of a fast motor car getting into bad driving habits.

Pieces of the Puzzle

A person is sitting down at a table with all the pieces of a puzzle on the table before him. The task is to complete the puzzle. The intelligent person may complete that puzzle rather quickly.

When all the pieces of the puzzle are given there is a skill in seeing how they fit together.

But in most situations the pieces of the puzzle are not given. You have to find and select the pieces. Most situations are open-ended not closed-ended.

The intelligence needed to find and select the pieces is not the same as the intelligence needed to put pre-selected pieces together.

Intelligence may be very good at 'understanding' things but is not necessarily so good at 'designing' or 'doing' things. Different skills are needed for the different situations.

Intelligence as Potential

Like the engine of a motor car, intelligence is a potential. There may be a fast car with rather a bad driver. There may be a more humble car with a better driver.

The danger lies solely in believing that IQ-tested intelligence is enough and that it carries with it the needed thinking skills. This conclusion is easy to reach in school where many of the tasks are very similar to those given in IQ tests. The real world may, however, be different.

Another danger is even more serious. This is the belief that those with a low performance on IQ tests cannot be good thinkers. This belief gives rise to a huge wastage of talent.

Given the right 'thinking tools' even those of relatively low IQ intelligence can do very well indeed, as we shall see later.

Less intelligent youngsters may not fully understand the 'game' that is expected of them at school, so they do poorly.

On a youngster's first day at school someone should sit that youngster down and tell him or her that the 'game' at school is to 'guess what the teacher wants'. With this simple clarification everyone would do much better at school – especially the poor performers.

Develop Potential

We need to acknowledge the importance of intelligence as a 'potential' and then we need to seek to develop that potential. This may involve the deliberate and direct teaching of thinking skills. There is a danger that such skills get taught only to the less intelligent, who are seen to benefit so greatly from such skills.

It is a mistake to assume that intelligent people are necessarily good thinkers.

INFORMATION

Thinking is never a substitute for information.

We need all the information we can get.

Two thousand years ago China was far ahead of the rest of the world in science and technology. They had gunpowder, rockets and many other things long before the rest of the world. Had China continued at the same rate of progress it would easily be the dominant power in the world today. But it did not continue. Progress came to a dead end. Why?

The scholars started to believe that they could move from certainty (fact) to certainty without any need for the messiness of 'possibility'. So they never developed the possibility system: hypothesis, speculation, imagination, etc. Progress came to a dead end.

Exactly the same thing is happening today in the West. Because of the excellence of our computers we are starting to believe that all you need to do is to collect and collate information. That information will do your thinking for you. That information will make your decisions, design your strategy and indicate the way forward.

This is much more dangerous than most people realise.

Thinking is needed to interpret the information in different ways.

Thinking is needed to put information together to design value.

Thinking is needed to see where to get more information.

Thinking is not a substitute for information but information is not a substitute for thinking.

Search Not Think

Youngsters given computers and Internet connections have a huge world opened up for them. This is a great privilege. There is a danger, however, that youngsters start to believe that you do not need to think. All you need to do is to 'search' and somewhere you will find that answer.

This is a difficult point. Everyone does not need to re-invent the wheel for him and herself. There is much useful information available that can save a lot of thinking.

What is important is that as we develop the search abilities we should at the same time develop the 'thinking' abilities.

The combination of thinking and information is most powerful.

School and Information

A large part of school is taken up with information. This is for two very practical reasons and two less so.

The first practical reason is that there is a lot of information around. It is there and it is relatively easy to teach. So as school is a sort of 'baby-sitting' exercise the information fills up time. The pupils are busy. The teacher is busy. The parents are happy.

The second practical reason is that information is easy to test. Does the pupil remember the information he or she is supposed to know? Marks and grades can be given. These are believed to be good motivators to get the pupils to work harder – directly or through the parents.

The third reason is that the information is there and has always been taught traditionally. In the UK children leave school knowing the names of most of Henry VIII's wives and even the date of the Treaty of Utrecht. Yet they have no ideas how the corner shop works or how value is created in society.

The fourth reason is the unfortunate belief that teaching information is a way of teaching thinking. This is a dangerous mistake since it blocks the direct teaching of thinking as a skill.

Certain skills of presentation and argument may accompany the teaching of information but these are only a very tiny part of practical real-life thinking.

Necessary but not Enough

If a chef spends so much time making elaborate pastries that he has no time to make a decent sauce that does not mean that the pastries are bad or even a waste of time. It simply means that time must be made available for the sauces.

There is no substitute for information. We need as much as we can get. But we need thinking as well. The skill of thinking does not arise from teaching more and more information. Unless you can teach the right answer to every conceivable situation, then the skill of thinking is needed.

THINKING

Thinking is the most fundamental of all human abilities.

The quality of our future will depend directly on the quality of our thinking.

There are few who would challenge the importance of 'thinking'.

So why do we not teach thinking explicitly and directly in our schools?

There are a number of possible reasons, which are listed below. There may be others not included here.

I am aware that there are several schools which do now teach thinking explicitly.

There are even whole countries, like Venezuela, where it is on the curriculum. By and large, however, most schools do not teach thinking explicitly.

The reasons below are not given in order of importance or even probability.

1. Thinking is not necessary.
    You are taught what to do in any situation and then you do what you should do. This is like workers on an assembly line. They do what they are expected to do.
    While this approach has some merit, it would be impossible to teach all situations and varieties of situations. In a changing world this is even more impossible.

2.   Information is enough.
      God cannot think because God has
      complete information outside of
      time and cannot move from one
      thought to a better one. So if we
      teach information and also how to
      get information (from the Internet,
      etc.) then the need for thinking is
      much reduced.
      Information without thinking is not
      enough. We need information but
      we also need thinking to see how to
      assess the information, how to use it
      and what further information might
      help.

3.   We already teach thinking.
      Because it seems so inconceivable
      that schools do not teach thinking,

there is a claim that they do. This claim is valid – up to a point. Some aspects of thinking are indeed taught. This includes the sorting of information, some analysis and the presentation of arguments.

This is all very valuable but is only a small part of the thinking needed in real life.

When my work was being used in Bulgaria they asked a nine-year-old girl from Plovdiv if she used the 'thinking tools' in real life. She replied:

'I use them all the time in real life. I even use them outside life – in school.'

John Edwards in Australia was teaching science to his pupils. He decided to teach less science and some thinking instead. His students did much better in their science exams than they had ever done.

In Argentina a school using my methods did so well in the national exams that they were investigated for cheating. Their results were so far out of line with the results of other schools.

I would not deny that schools do teach some thinking but I would suggest that it can be taught more powerfully and much more broadly than in the context of information skills.

4. Thinking cannot be taught.
    This is probably the main reason. There is the innocent ignorance of teachers who simply do not know

how thinking can be taught. Their teacher training colleges did not teach them how to teach thinking so they do not know that it can be done.

There is the dogmatic ignorance of those pundits who take the rigid position that thinking is a matter of inborn intelligence and cannot be taught.

This last view is simply absurd nonsense as the results of teaching thinking have become obvious.

Our Software for Thinking

Around the world there are thousands of people writing software for computers.

How much effort have we made to write software for the human mind?

The answer is that, outside of mathematics, we have made no effort at all for about 2,400 years.

Why?

Because the excellence of the software designed by the GG3 (Greek Gang of Three) has seemed so perfect that there was no need for new software.

Socrates was trained as a Sophist. He was concerned with dialectic or argument.

Plato was influenced by the mathematician Pythagoras and he believed that just as there were ultimate truths in mathematics so there should by ultimate truths everywhere.

Aristotle introduced his 'box logic'. Define some categories or classifications. Then you judged whether something was in this box or not in the box (it could not be halfway or anywhere else). Then you knew all about that thing from the label on the box.

During the Renaissance Greek thinking (GG3) came into Europe through the Arabs in Spain. The people running schools and universities in Europe were largely Church people.

They were not interested in:

Perceptual thinking: because all the starting perceptions in theology were pre-determined.

Creative thinking: because there was no need and it could be dangerous.

Constructive thinking: because the operations of the Church were structured and strategic thinking was only for the top level.

Operational thinking: because that was not what the Church was about.

The interest of those Church thinkers was in logic, truth and argument. These were needed to prove heretics wrong.

That was the basis for thinking in education and it has continued so, through tradition, to this day. It is a very difficult continuity to break because any advisors come from within the tradition and so defend it.

Perceptual Thinking

This is a very, very important part of thinking – and almost completely neglected. No matter how good our logic may be the end result will depend on the starting perceptions. If these perceptions are false and inadequate the answer will be rubbish – even if the logic is impeccable.

Gödel's theorem shows how from within a system, logic can never prove the starting points. The starting point is perception.

The CoRT programme (Cognitive Research Trust), now widely used in schools, is all about improving perception.

This sort of thinking, taught by the Holst Group in the UK to participants on the government New Deal programme for unemployed youngsters, increased the employment rate five hundred per cent. A year later ninety-six per cent were still in employment. The 'thinking' was only taught for five hours.

This sort of thinking was taught by David Lane, the principal of the Hungerford Guidance Centre in London (for youngsters too violent to be taught in normal schools), to the violent youngsters. In a twenty-year follow-up he showed that the rate of actual criminal conviction for those taught thinking was only one tenth of the rate for those not taught thinking.

In the Karee platinum mine in South Africa there used to be two hundred and ten fights every month between the seven tribes working there. Susan Mackie and Donalda Dawson taught this thinking to the totally illiterate miners who had never been to school even for one day in their lives. The fights dropped from two hundred and ten to just four.

I use these examples because most people believe that bad behaviour depends on emotions and man's basic instincts, and that these cannot be touched by any amount of thinking.

This is simply not true. Logic will never touch emotions but perceptual thinking will. If you see things in a different way your reaction is different.

What was taught to all the people in the above examples was direct thinking – not morals or attitudes or values.

Research by David Perkins at Harvard University confirms the importance of perception. He showed that ninety per cent of the errors in thinking are errors of perception. Logic accounts for a minor ten per cent.

Yet we continue to believe, as we have done for centuries, that thinking is all about logic.

As I mentioned earlier in the book, some people are very good at solving a puzzle if all the pieces are put out in front of them. But that is not practical in real life. It is perception that chooses and decides on the pieces.

No amount of excellence in logic will make up for a deficit in perception.

Critical Thinking

This is a useful part of thinking. But it is only part of thinking.

Our traditional (GG3) thinking is all about analysing a situation and identifying standard elements. Then we provide the standard answer to these standard elements.

So Ben S. Bernanke in Washington (head of the Federal Reserve Bank) looks at the economic situation. If he recognises inflation the standard response is to raise interest rates. If he recognises recession then the standard response is to lower interest rates. There are serious flaws in the thinking – but it is traditional.

The word 'critical' comes from the Greek word, 'kritikos', for judge. It is judgement thinking. Is this right or wrong? Does this fit in this box or does it not? Is this consistent with what went before, or not? Etc.

I want to emphasise again that this is a valuable part of thinking but by no means enough. What is left out is:

Creative thinking
Perceptual thinking
Design thinking
Operational thinking
Exploratory thinking, etc.

Attitudes and Tools

Attitudes are very weak and do not transfer. Attitudes are like itineraries set up by a travel agent. You use them but they do not lodge in your mind.

A tool is a specific mental operation. The OPV tool in the CoRT programme reminds the thinker to consider the thinking of the other party (for example in a fight). OPV stands for 'Other People's View'.

Because it is an acronym it has a place in the brain. This is just like the names of vegetables, which also have a place in the brain. You do not ask for 'a shiny, round red vegetable which is good for salads'. You ask for 'a tomato'.

The acronyms are an important part of the 'tool approach'. There have been schools were one teacher used the acronyms but another teacher disdained the 'phoney acronyms' and tried to teach attitudes. It did not work. The second teacher quickly came back to using the acronyms. That is the way the brain works.

Creativity

While aesthetic judgement may play a key part in the art world, there is no mystique or magic about 'idea creativity'.

Idea creativity is a mental skill that can be taught and practiced as formally as mathematics. This is what lateral thinking is about.

The brain works as a self-organising information system. Such systems make patterns. Patterning systems are always asymmetric (the path from A to B is not the same as the path from B to A). Both humour and creativity depend on this asymmetry.

The formal techniques of lateral thinking (challenge, concept extraction, concept fan, provocation, random entry, etc.) can all be learned, practiced and used deliberately.

One afternoon Caroline Ferguson in South Africa set up a group of work-shops for the steel company ISCOR. Using just one of the formal tools of lateral thinking the groups generated 21,000 new ideas. It took nine months just to sort through the ideas. This goes far beyond inspiration or brainstorming.

Argument

We have the tradition of argument designed by the GG3. We use the method in parliament and in the courts of law.

It is an extremely primitive, crude and inefficient way of exploring a subject (if this is the need).

In a court of law if the prosecuting lawyer thinks of a point that would help the defence case, is that lawyer going to raise that point? Of course not. If the defence lawyer thinks of a point that would help the prosecution, is the defence lawyer going to raise that point? Of course not.

The process is one of 'case-making', not of exploring the subject.

In argument you must start with a 'position' – otherwise you cannot argue. In exploration, you explore first and reach a position at the end of the exploration.

In argument there is no design effort. You are arguing A against not-A or against B. There is no energy going into designing the possibility of C, D or E.

Argument is about egos, emotions, attack, defend, win, lose, etc.

Parallel Thinking
An alternative to argument is now becoming widely used around the world.

It is used in the primitive highlands of Papua New Guinea and in the top economic discussions in Washington. It is used by four-year-olds in schools and by top executives in many of the world's best-known corporations.

A company in Finland used to spend thirty days on their multi-national project discussions. Using the Six Hats method they now do it in two days.

Juries in the USA are being taught the method and are reaching unanimous decisions very quickly.

MDC, a corporation in Canada, did a careful costing and showed that in the first year they used the Six Hats they saved $20 million.

People are beginning to realise that while argument has its place, it is a very poor way of exploring a subject. The Six Hats method is being used more and more because it gets the best thinking from all those present.

Under the White Hat everyone focuses on information. What do we have? What do we need? How are we going to get the information we need?

Under the Red Hat everyone is allowed to express their emotions, intuitions and feelings of the moment.

Under the Black Hat everyone focuses on the dangers, problems, weaknesses and downsides of an idea, and also on any faults in logic or thinking.

Under the Yellow Hat everyone looks for benefits and values and how the idea could be made to happen.

Under the Green Hat everyone looks for new ideas, further alternatives and possibilities. Under this hat everyone is expected to make a creative effort – or keep quiet. People do not like keeping quiet so they make a creative effort – and often surprise themselves.

The Blue Hat is the organising hat. This hat determines the focus and the desired outcome. This hat sets the sequence of use of the hats and also the discipline of use. This hat puts together the outcome and decides the next step in the thinking.

Range

I have taught thinking to four-year-olds and to ninety-year-olds (at Roosevelt University).

I have taught thinking to Down syndrome youngsters and to Nobel Prize winners.

I have taught thinking to illiterate miners in South Africa and to top executives at some of the world's largest corporations: IBM, Shell, NTT, Nokia, etc.

I have taught thinking to cricket teams and to orchestras.

Love It

Children love thinking. They love the opportunity to use their minds and to come up with new ideas.

In one school the main punishment for bad behaviour was that you would not be allowed to go to the thinking lessons.

For a youngster every idea is an achievement – and an opportunity to show off.

Again and again children choose 'thinking' as their favourite subject.